BULLY-FREE ZONE !

Written by Ann

Illustrated by Juliana Paiva

BULLY - FREE ZONE

Copyright © 2023 Ann

All Rights Reserved.

ISBN: 979-8-89109-722-3 (Paperback)
ISBN: 979-8-89109-748-3 (Hardcover)
ISBN: 979-8-89109-723-0 (Ebook)

AUTHOR'S NOTE

Coach Brittany Plumeri: I feel as if I was running a marathon and could hear you shouting and chanting my name, saying, "Ann, you got this! You can do it!" a challenge you inspired me to complete. Thank you.

Sheri Wall: My editor works like a beautician. Thank you for your creativity in bringing my story to light and giving it the best look ever – and the lift it needed. Thank you.

"Who can tell me the answer to number two?"
asks Ms. Murphy during math class.
"Mike?"

"T-t-t-t-ten."

Luis and Anthony laugh and stutter under their breath.
"T-t-t-totally awesome."

Mike knocks over their books as he rushes back to his seat.

During English, Lisa and Pam giggle and point at Mike's worn clothes. "Maybe he's homeless."

"Stop being so mean!" Mara sighs.

"He's mean to us too," says Luis.
"He's always on his computer making fun
of us in memes. He made fun of my haircut."

Matthew decides to speak up.
"Those memes are really not cool, Mike."

"Seriously, they are mean
and hurt our feelings."

Mike just laughs as he heads to lunch.

Mike wishes he had a snack cake.
He decides to snatch Daniel's cake.
"Hey! That's mine; give it back!"

Daniel and Mathew both jump to their feet.
Mike looks from one to the other.
Daniel realizes that Mike seems a little scared.

Smack! Mike smashes the pack into Daniel's hand

Daniel calmly opens the wrapper.
"Here, you can have one."
"Thanks. I like these smash cakes."

As Mike turns to leave, Daniel and Mathew know they should try to help Mike, but they're not sure how.

"Mike, bullying back doesn't make you cool,"
Mathew explains.

"I know; I don't want to be cool. I just want to be friends with everyone, but they are always mean to me, and it hurts. My mom says to ignore them, but I can't. I want to show them how I feel when they are mean to me." Mike looks down at his sneakers and holds in his tears.

"I don't think everyone realizes you want to be friends," adds Daniel. "What if there was some way to show them?"

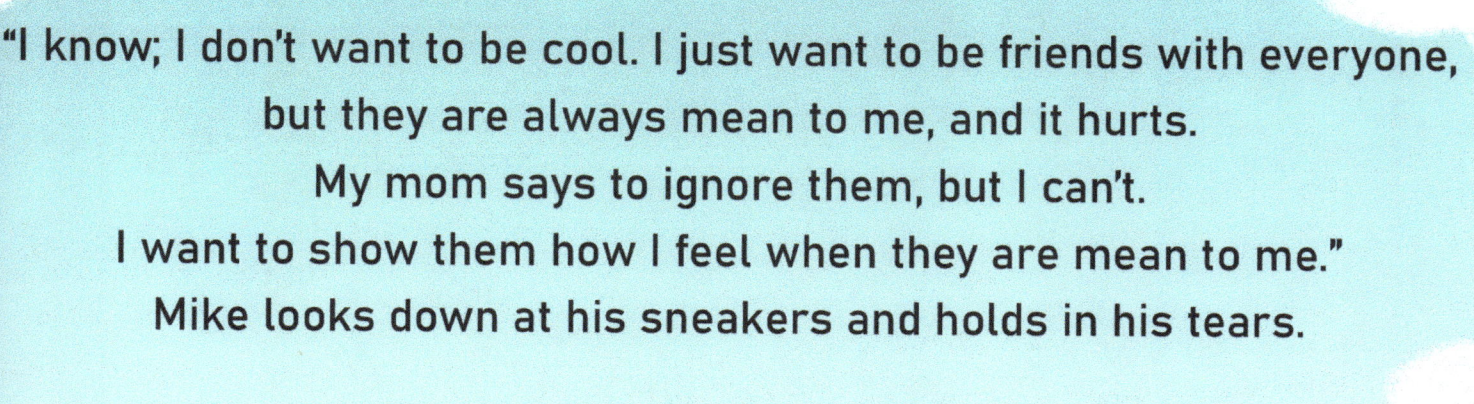

Mike's eyes go wide.
"I think I have an idea!"

As computers start humming the next day of school,
there's a new meme on the home screen.
It has everyone's picture with
"Let's Be Friends" across the top.

"Mike, did you do this?" asks Daniel.
Mike shyly grins.

"Who else could have? Mike is our very own computer whiz!" says Mathew.

"Thanks, Mike!" says Luis.
"This is way better than the other ones!"
Slowly, the students are kinder to each other, and
things get better for everyone in
Ms. Murphy's class.

Everything in Coach Cook's PE class
was going well...well, until Melvin arrived.

When Mike misses a shot,
Melvin isn't happy. "Thanks, loser!"

"STOP!" Mathew's voice is so loud that everyone is still and quiet.
"We don't allow bullying here."

"And we want to keep it that way!"
Daniel announces.

Mara agrees.
"Yes, we want to keep it that way!"

"I'm sorry," Melvin says nervously.
His cheeks turn bright red.

"I didn't mean that, Mike. You've got some good moves.
Maybe you can teach me?"
"Yeah, okay. I can do that."

Coach Cook blows his whistle. Everyone huddles around him.
"I am proud of what I heard today." Instead of running laps,
how about we work together to make
a sign for the school entrance?"

The class erupted, "Woo Hoo, let's do it!"
They hurried off to gather supplies so they
could start right away.

The classmates worked hard until
the sign was finished.

www.ingramcontent.com/pod-product-compliance
Lightning Source LLC
Chambersburg PA
CBHW041157120626
46547CB00020B/3244